Dec 13 - 2014

*Dedicated to my readers
and supporters:*

Thank you for honoring
you with life's gift of
deeper sexual intimacy.

TICKLE MY TUSH

Mild-to-Wild Analplay Adventures for Everybooty

Dr. Sadie Allison
Illustrated by Steve Lee

ticklekitty®
go love.

Tickle Kitty, Inc.
3701 Sacramento Street #107
San Francisco, CA 94118
United States
Fax: (415) 876-1900

Editor: J. Croker Norge
Illustrator: Steve Lee
Page Layout & Design: inktankdesign.com
Author Photographer: Richard Marz
Cover Photographer: Jazmin J.

PLEASE NOTE

This book is intended for educational and entertainment purposes only. Neither the Author, Illustrator, nor Publisher is responsible for the use or misuse of any sexual techniques or devices discussed here, or for any loss, damage, injury or ailment caused by reliance on any information contained in this book. Please use common sense. The illustrations in this book depict couples who are in faithful, monogamous relationships. Readers who are not monogamous, or who have not been tested for STIs (sexually transmitted infections), are strongly urged to employ the safer sex practices in Chapter 3. If you have any health issues or other concerns, you should consult a qualified healthcare professional or licensed therapist BEFORE trying any techniques or devices. Please read Chapter 3 for tips on safer sex, and consult a physician or a qualified healthcare professional if you have any further questions. Be sure to read and carefully follow all instructions that come with any sexual aids you decide to use. The mention of any product or service in this book does not constitute an endorsement.

TICKLE MY TUSH

Mild-to-Wild Analplay Adventures for Everybooty

Come Inside

ForePlay

Anal. Sex.

Funny how these two little words together can create such an uproar.

That's no surprise, of course, after enduring centuries of mystery, hearsay, taboo—and that predictable *eeew* of the uninformed.

Yet, you did pick up this book, and to you I say, *welcome!* I'm here to unmask the mysteries, toss away those taboos, and clear up any leftover misinformation so you can explore everything you like—up close and personal—or from a safe (yet exciting) distance.

The decision to try buttplay is entirely up to you. No pressure, no judgement, no shame—and best of all, you'll discover there's really nothing "wrong" with it. Frankly, it's one of the most intimate acts of lovemaking you'll ever try.

Yet buttplay is not a spur-of-the-moment decision either, because it takes preparation, responsibility, safety and unselfishness to enjoy it to its fullest. After all, it's *your* body, *your* feelings, *your* pleasure, *your* adventure.

So nestle in, relax, and let me guide you on a sexual journey that's unlike anything you've ever experienced. I'll make sure you're ready, comfortable, informed, safe and wildly aroused. And, oh yeah: I promise to be gentle.

Come spin the analplay decision wheel

Most of us already know where we stand on analplay. You do, and so does your lover. But have the two of you honestly answered the biggest question of all: Are your positions one and the same?

Over time, I've discovered there are really only three choices on the Analplay Decision Wheel:

1. I Dunno...?
2. Gung Ho!
3. Hell No!

You could easily find yourselves in an analplay mismatch. One of you is red-hot—the other's not. Or both of you are open-minded, but feeling confused or uncertain. Or here's a shocker I'm seeing more and more: the mount*er* suddenly realizes he's now being eyed as the mount*ee*! To all of you I say: let me help you find your common ground.

But first, may I ask a favor—no matter where you stand on analplay?

Please keep reading, at least one more page.

Why? Because this book isn't about analplay...exclusively.

It's about that entire erogenous zone that follows you wherever you go. (You know, the one you've admired in others as they're walking away—and vice-versa!)

If you haven't yet explored that *entire* region of eros-sensitivity—you and your lover are overlooking some highly sensual butt foreplay, as well as some hot, tantalizing *ohhh-so-close*-but-not-quite penetration thrills. And I'm right here to guide you, at your own pace and comfort.

Butt wait...there's more!

Yes, there's no shortage of bad puns, and I promise I'll try and hold them back.

The truth is, I've deliberately written this book from mild to wild. This means you may find the first few chapters terribly exciting, and the next few chapters simply terrible. Or you may wish this book would never end.

The real beauty of mild to wild is you get to choose the erotic techniques to your liking—and (caution: unavoidable bad pun ahead) leave the rest behind.

What better way to spice up your relationship, revive a lagging sex life, or add daring new adventures to your pleasure repertoire. There are two butts in your bedroom, right? Just keep in mind that pleasing your lover with these intensely intimate joys means they can easily come right back at ya!

Sound like a plan? You've got nothing to lose, and new intimacy to gain. At your own pace, on your own terms, and only as far as you desire, of course.

X's and O's,

Dr. Sadie
America's Pleasure Coach

1 Butts Up?

Why in the world would anyone desire anal sex?

Aside from the one-track fascination of the "Gung Ho!," it turns out that more and more straight couples are now exploring this highly erotic adventure. In fact, it's confirmed by recent health and sexuality surveys.

And if anyone in your town happens to be offering seminars on safe analplay, make your reservations early: they're selling out. Even the number of analplay questions that people email to *Tickle Kitty* are on the rise.

Yet perhaps the leading indicator of analplay enthusiasm is showing its biggest jump in history. Sextoy manufacturers note a rise in sales for all kinds of quality, buzzy, curvy toys designed exclusively for anal pleasure—now widely available for purchase in mainstream consumer outlets.

But enough about everyone else. What about *you?* What if you're unsure about analplay, leaning away, or even running away? What if you're intrigued by some of it, but not all of it? And what if your lover's backdoor "hints" are getting louder and more impassioned?

Do you ignore—or explore?

Skip the how, and grasp the why

Are you up for exploring new adventures? Then take a deep breath, open your mind, and try to forget the subject of this book. *Really.*

Now, with all your preconceived notions cleared, and no one looking over your shoulder (except perhaps your lover!), check off all of your wants and desires as a couple:

Our Wants & Desires Checklist

Fill it out together and feel free to add your own.

☐ **Deeper intimacy.**

Enhance the emotional connection I crave.

☐ **Sexual exploration.**

Expanding boundaries to new horizons really excites me.

☐ **Super orgasms.**

I love 'em eye-popping, sheet-grabbing, larger-than-life.

☐ **Table turning.**

I get excited not just from giving, but from receiving.

☐ **Partner pleasing.**

I get off sending my lover into full pleasure orbit.

☐ **Adventure seeking.**

Mysterious new sensations + acting naughty = big thrills.

☐ _____

☐ _____

☐ _____

Did you check more than two? Four? All?

Congratulations! You can be completely fulfilled and emotionally satisfied for the rest of your life *if you never have anal sex.* On the other hand, you may be surprised to discover that the survey you just completed is also a checklist of the top reasons women and men say they enjoy analplay.

Now that you know the *why,* it's important you know the *why not.*

When you should *not* get involved

As with everything people enjoy in life, there's moderation on one hand, and recklessness on the other. And drawing a line between the two is essential to your health and safety.

The reasons are ultra-clear: Anal sex requires mutual consent, trust, communication, preparation and a lot of safety precautions.

If you ever feel you are being pressured into this act, STOP! Anal sex can be loaded with physical and emotional risks for you.

Remember: this book is written for trusting, mature couples—and is based on safety first, pleasure second. Please be sure to do what's best for YOU.

So...are you ready?

A simple, honest, curiosity-seeking *yes* will take you as far as you wish to go. You'll start off with loving pleasures you may already know, enhancing them safely and erotically—from mild to wild— along this guided path:

♥ **MILD.** Start by exploring what's perhaps the most ignored pleasure zone—the *entire* backside. You'll learn sensual new touches, massages and other erotic joys that involve *no penetration whatsoever.* You two can enjoy surprising buttplay pleasures you may never have dreamed of!

♥ **WILDER.** To really rev your engines, come zero-in on that center of love, a tiny spot rippling with zillions of erotic pleasure receptors waiting to thrill you like never before. Soft fingertip play, with or without some modest penetration, could rocket you to the most satisfying pleasures you've ever experienced.

♥ **WILDEST.** Discover the how-to secrets of pleasurable penetration—the preparation, positions, safety and thrills— for one *or both* of you. You'll also reach into today's toy chest of pleasure, pulling out specially designed analplay sextoys to excite and delight you.

So are you mildest? Wildest? Or somewhere in between? It's all perfectly fine, as long as you start slowly and move forward at your own pace.

And one last tip: read this book together. In bed.

You'll not only make these erotic discoveries simultaneously—you won't have to wait very long to try 'em!

A word about words

Wouldn't you agree, that some of the hesitancy you may feel toward analplay has a lot to do with the hideous language we've been given to describe it?

Anus—*eek!* Sphincter—*oy!* Feces—*yuck!*

On the other hand, there's a rich abundance of slang available too, like asshole, chocolate highway, bone smuggler. Go ahead: try saying THAT in your sexiest voice without laughing!

After vigorous debate, Tickle Kitty's editors unanimously agreed to swap many of this act's unappetizing language with more enlightened words designed to pulsate—not repulse. Hopefully you'll agree it's a change for the better:

Dr. Sadie's Official Analplay Translator

(Because this is a sex book—not a textbook!)

OUT	IN
Anus	**A-spot**
Sphincter (A-spot muscles)	**O-rings**
Anal canal	**Pleasure inch**
Rectum	**Pleasure tunnel**
Anal sex	**Analplay or Buttplay**
Feces	**Poop or Color**
Ass	**Tush, Booty or Butt**
Analingus	**Rimming or Licking**
Intergluteal cleft (buttcrack)	**Butt cleavage**
Perineum (sensitive area between A-spot & genitals)	**Taint**

Is analplay only for straight couples?

Did you do a double-take? While many lovers— gay and straight—have always enjoyed anal sex, it's historically been seen mostly as a gay act. That's why I created this analplay guide for heterosexuals: because straight guys are often uncomfortable with man-on-man imagery. This can easily cost them the promise of pleasure, no matter how much their wives or girlfriends insist to the contrary. To you guys I say, go ahead and explore—your heterosexuality is secure! (Turn to page 14 if you don't believe me.) But since all butts are created equal, the information in this book can help anyone—no matter what their sexual orientation is. That's why it says "Adventures for Everybooty" on the cover!

Dr. Sadie Sez

2

Frequently Assed Questions

More questions seem to arise from buttplay than any other erotic adventure. But that's what happens whenever taboos around sex lift and pleasure goes more mainstream (yet it's still smart to ask!).

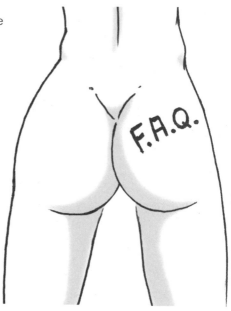

F.A.Q.

Uh, is analplay a natural or unnatural act?

It's as natural as nature.

Humans have been enjoying anal pleasures as long as there have been eager penises, curious fingers and welcoming butts. Its acceptance has varied widely among people and civilizations throughout history, from taboo to *whoo-hoo!*

You may have heard people say, "It's an exit, not an entrance!" But isn't that as silly as saying a vagina is only for giving birth?

Ahem, isn't it kinda gay?

Sure, if you're *already* gay. But if you're a heterosexual man, nope—it's actually impossible when you're with someone of the opposite sex.

Note: it's the gender of your partner—not the sexual activity—that defines your sexual orientation.

What about, *uhh*, poop?

Good question, and it's probably not what you're thinking.

If you're playing on the mild side, it's no concern at all. And if you venture to the wild side, it's really no concern IF you follow the body cleansing and prepping directions in Chapter 4.

For peace of mind, simply be prepared. Use an old set of sheets, or spread a large dark towel over the bed. Keep scented personal wipes within reach—as well as a handy bag to dispose of them. And if you do find a tiny bit of color, don't be alarmed—just wipe it up. You can share a laugh over it later as you celebrate the most heart-pounding sex of your life.

What if he's well-endowed?

Thankfully, you can accept more than you may realize. To ease your mind, test drive a dildo that's close to the girth of your lover's penis. Is he extra hung? You've got the depth you need as well, with room to expand. Or, simply choose positions that shorten penetration, which you'll find in Chapter 13. But whatever you do, be sure to apply even more lube on yourself, and all over his entire shaft.

Yikes, will it hurt?

Nope! Not if you're doing it right.

Sometimes the sensations are described as "mild discomfort" or a pleasurable "hurts so good" feeling. Most negative sensations are chalked up to the learning curve, and are usually overcome with time and practice.

Playing around back there takes some getting used to, because the A-spot isn't nearly as elastic as the vagina—so the safety precautions and pleasure techniques in this book are unique to this erogenous zone. By preheating your lover and following this advice, you'll more likely come to describe it as erotic gliding, sensations of fullness, and breathtaking stimulation.

Should I be hesitant if I've felt pain before?

Pain during anal sex is most often the result of two people not knowing how to safely engage in this act. If your motivation is pure, your lover is compassionate, and the time is right, try exploring analplay slowly, so you can feel in control, safe and relaxed. If you're having discomfort—stop, either for a few minutes, or until another time. Remember, it's your decision to proceed. But if you follow the advice in this book, you could easily see your hesitancy disappear.

How can I be sure analplay is for me?

Luckily, there's a no-pressure way to find out—and you even get to leave your lover completely out of it! When you're all alone, just lube up *your own* index finger and try it out yourself.

Aside from adding a potential new dimension to your masturbation repertoire, you'll start becoming comfortable with the rush of these pleasurable new sensations. If they're exciting to you, your lover's gentle touch will probably be *even more* thrilling.

And because you've now become much more self-aware, your fingers are fully empowered to return waves of excitement and pleasure to your lover as well. Just be sure to read about safer sex practices in Chapter 3 before you dive in.

Is anal sex safe when I'm pregnant?

If your physician gives you the okay, then enjoy! Just go slowly, and be sure you follow the safer sex practices in Chapter 3, including condom-wearing. If penetration feels like too much, limit your fun to butt massage and fingertip pleasures. And if hemorrhoids have become an issue, wait until they calm down first.

Can I *really* orgasm from analplay?

Some people can! Between the zillions of sensitive nerve endings surrounding the A-spot, and how you angle to stimulate her G-spot or his "He-spot" (prostate gland), plus the exotic pressures you create inside, you can actually trigger powerful orgasms. Want to skyrocket your odds? Simply add in some well-timed clitoral, penile or prostate stimulation.

Yet focusing single-mindedly on orgasming is the best way NOT to come.

Your best bet: start with a more sensual approach, and enjoy the journey itself. Focus on the pleasures of massaging, touching, kissing, licking, and some of the wilder adventures, like trying a vibrating toy for over-the-top sensations.

And what if you still don't come? It's no big deal. After all, you've got plenty of other pleasure moves to detonate those orgasmic build-ups!

How do I let my lover know I want buttplay?

Start an open, honest conversation. Bring up your desire when you're both in a relaxed mood (not in the frenzy of foreplay!). Stay positive, and explain it's about mutual discovery and new intimacy, and that it doesn't mean anything's wrong with your love life. Flesh out any fears that may be holding your lover back (most of them will be answered in this book). Be prepared for any reaction, and be respectful if the answer is no.

If you're on the receiving end of this talk, try listening before reacting. Your partner is going out on a limb, and you'll learn a lot by not rolling your eyes or slamming the door. Don't assume this desire has anything to do with sexual dissatisfaction. More than likely, it's because you've got a good, trusting comfort level with each other, and your lover is ready to explore a deeper intimacy with you. Not yet? Table the discussion for another time.

3 Safety First

You've surely heard about the dangers of unprotected sex—perhaps so often that you've started to tune it all out.

Yet these risks still apply to everyone, every time.

Even you.

But here's good news: safer sex doesn't have to slow you down. In fact, you'll find it actually enhances the mood, since you'll both spend far less time worrying—and far more time loving.

So put your most powerful sex organ to work for you: your brain. Practice the safety precautions in this chapter. Your health—and life—depend on it.

Safety Savvy #1: Get smart about STIs, STDs & HIV/AIDS

They once whispered about someone having a "social disease." Then they changed it to "VD" for venereal disease (named in some sort of odd tribute to Venus, the Roman goddess of love). Now anything you catch through sexual contact is known as an STI or an STD. But what's the difference?

An STI (sexually transmitted infection) is a hidden viral or bacterial infection that's showing no symptoms—yet. And even though a person with an STI may not know they have one, *they can still spread it.*

An STD (sexually transmitted disease) is simply an STI that's revealed itself by showing symptoms.

STIs and STDs can be spread through oral, vaginal and anal sex. Most *bacterial* STIs can be treated and cured—and many *viral* STIs can be treated and subdued. But leaving *any* STI or STD untreated can lead to serious complications and consequences you don't want.

The list of potential STIs reads like a Who's Who of Oh No: gonorrhea, syphilis, hepatitis B and C, herpes, human papilloma virus (HPV), chlamydia and others. Of course, the most serious STI of all is the viral infection HIV/AIDS. As with *any* intimate sexual contact with an exchange of bodily fluid, there is risk of contracting any of these diseases *if your partner is infected.* This risk increases during anal sex, because the very thin lining of the A-spot is so delicate, it can tear more easily, giving these microscopic villains a way in. And the best way to prevent tearing is by applying plenty of slippery lube—every time.

Important: if you and your partner have just tested free of all STIs, and you've both agreed to be 100 percent monogamous— then *and only then* should you ever consider engaging in anal sex without protection.

CAUTION

UNPROTECTED SEX—EVEN ONCE—WHETHER ORAL, VAGINAL OR ANAL CAN POSE SERIOUS HEALTH RISKS TO YOU AND YOUR PARTNER. ALWAYS USE BARRIER PROTECTION AND FOLLOW THE SAFER SEX PRACTICES IN THIS BOOK.

Safety Savvy #2: Safeguard yourself with barrier protection

The most famous type of thin barrier protection—the condom—has been part of lovemaking for centuries. Originally made of linen (ouch!), today you have dozens of sensation-enhancing options that comfortably fit every penis shape, too.

Thin barriers also come in flat squares, finger cots and gloves—all designed to keep germs out and pleasures in. They smooth-out fingernails and rough skin for a ride that glides—and stop germs from sneaking in through cuts and cuticles on fingers as well.

♥ **SLIDE ON A CONDOM.** Whatever you call them—condoms, rubbers, jimmy-hats—these thin, heat-transmitting, full-length penis barriers provide you with the most effective protection to keep STIs from entering either of you. They're also highly effective at preventing unwanted pregnancies and UTIs (urinary tract infections). Condoms today are inexpensive and readily available in a variety of materials, sizes, textures and colors—so choose your pleasure!

♥ **UNROLL A FINGER COT.** Also known as a "finger condom," finger cots are designed to roll down and fit snuggly over just one finger, for your single fingerplay adventures. They're available in a variety of water-tight materials including latex, nitrile rubber and vinyl.

♥ **SPREAD OUT A DENTAL DAM.** Place one of these tissue-sized ultra-thin flat squares of micro-thin latex or polyurethane over your lover's A-spot—then lick all you like! Choose a flavored one that's sweet on the tongue-side, and dab some water-based lube on the other side for extra sensation. (So you won't mix-up the sides, mark the mouth-side with an X—or draw a ♥ on it.)

♥ **SLIP INTO A GLOVE.** For full-coverage fun, try slipping your hand into a latex glove for a silky smoothness that minimizes friction and maximizes pleasure. Slather lots of water-based or silicone lube on the outside and let your fingers do the walking! For a visual treat, choose a fun color like pink or purple, or a sexy black.

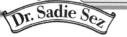

Don't let porn be your teacher

Do you know why porn actors go in so hard and fast? They preheat before the cameras ever start rolling. But you don't see that because in the visual world of adult entertainment, speed is king. So think twice before ever mimicking those moves—and slow down—because that's usually not what your lover likes or wants, Romeo.

Dr. Sadie Sez

The Condom Conundrum: Do's & Don'ts

DO'S!

Do! Stock up in advance

Do! Choose a pre-lubricated condom

Do! Use a size that fits properly

Do! Wear latex (or polyurethane if you're allergic)

Do! Add a drop of lube *inside* the condom to help prevent breakage

Do! Leave space at the tip when you roll it on

Do! Remember each fresh erection = fresh new condom

Do! Use lots of lube—always

DONT'S!

Don't! Use condoms with spermicides —like Nonoxynol-9

Don't! Wear lambskin condoms —they're virus permeable

Don't! Use household products like petroleum jelly or oil

Don't! Risk tearing a condom by opening the packet with your teeth

Don't! Leave condoms in sunlight, in wallet or glovebox

Don't! Use condoms after their expiration date

Don't! Use condoms if they look or smell bad out of the wrapper

Don't! Apply oil-based lubes on latex condoms

Safety Savvy #3: Warm it up

Preheating your lover is a prerequisite for safe analplay. Why? The A-spot takes longer to "get in the mood" than a penis or vagina. Going in too soon can hurt or injure your lover. Taking your time by warming up slowly and sensually can lead to exquisite pleasure and toe-curling orgasms.

Safety Savvy #4: Never double-dip

Once you've progressed to analplay, the vagina and mouth are both off-limits until you've thoroughly washed finger(s), sextoy, dildo or penis with anti-bacterial soap and warm water. This will keep you from introducing bacteria where it doesn't belong.

The slower you go, the faster you get there

It can be tough to ride the brakes when you're ready to zoom, but analplay is delicate play—especially when you're all revved up. As tough or as sexy as the receiver is on the outside, the inside is guaranteed to be tender, and needs to be slowly warmed and fully aroused first. However far you take your buttplay pleasures, let me repeat: The slower you go, the faster you get there. 'Nuf said.

Dr. Sadie Sez

Safety Savvy #5: Lube it up

Always slather plenty of slippery sex lubricant (and not just saliva) all over everything heading inside: fingers, sextoys, dildos and penis. Why? Humans aren't factory-equipped with anal lubrication glands, so there's no natural lubrication back there. This means it's entirely up to you to add a slippery coating to give your ride its glide. It's essential—or someone can get hurt. Seriously. Lube it up. A lot. Then reapply. Every time.

♥ **SILICONE.** Silicone lube offers a thicker consistency and stays slippery the longest. That's why it's ideal for buttplay. And since it doesn't wash off quickly, it's perfect for showerplay, too. (Caution: shower floor can get slippery.)

♥ **WATER-BASED.** Water-based lube has a thinner consistency but glides nicely, and cleans up easily. But since its slipperiness doesn't last as long as silicone lube, be sure to reapply often.

Do **not** use lubes with glycerin, flavorings or oil—which do not belong in your butt. And if you're new at analplay, say no to numbing or warming lubes, because they can dull or disguise any sensations of discomfort you'd want to know about.

Safety Savvy #6: Speak up—be honest

Practice the art of honest communication, and tell your lover when things are happening too fast, too rough, too deep, too whatever— or if you need to stop. You can also say when things feel exquisitely right, too. Either way, please speak up. Both of you.

Safety Savvy #7: Be a responsible lover

Knowing the right thing to do—and not doing it—is perhaps your biggest risk of all. For your sake, for your lover's sake, for your future's sake, take the wisdom in this chapter seriously. Be a hero—not a statistic. Protect yourself.

Cap the nightcaps

Too much alcohol and/or recreational drugs can make you a sloppy lover. Since analplay calls for care and communication, staying in the closer-to-sober zone enhances your enjoyment and helps ensure your safety through better judgement.

Dr. Sadie Sez

4 Heinie Hygiene

Question: What's sexier than a nice set of buns?

Answer: A nice set of buns you've trimmed, groomed and sexed-up just for your lover.

Now THAT'S *amore!*

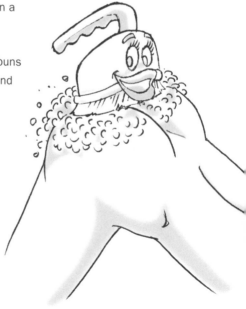

For starters, wash up down there!

If the sensual scent of roses, lavender or lilac lifts your spirits, imagine how relaxed 'n ready you'll feel when your soft buttocks remind your lover of a field of flowers—instead of just a field.

The solution couldn't be simpler: bathe! For ultra-clean confidence, scrub well with soap and a fresh washcloth. Don't miss an inch.

Better yet, start the party early and shower together! Now two sets of hot, clean buns will beckon like never before, leaving just one pressing question: Whose will be enjoyed first?

Solve the enema enigma

Do you need an enema before engaging in analplay? It would seem like you do—but you really don't.

Clearing the rectum ahead of time with a good bowel movement is a fine idea for peace of mind, but not always necessary. You might consider a high-fiber drink the day before to promote a healthy movement. And avoid heavy or gassy foods in the 24 hours leading up to the big event.

Of course, if you'd feel more relaxed, or you simply like enemas, then go ahead and indulge—it's fine.

Wash your hands thoroughly

Seeing a pair of dirty hands and untrimmed fingernails creeping toward you plays like a bad horror flick. Turn it into a love story by washing your hands thoroughly with anti-bacterial soap and water right before playtime. And use a fingernail scrub-brush to get underneath the nails. Now your soft, warm, clean-as-a-whistle fingers are ready to wiggle your lover to ecstasy.

Tame your fingernails

Fingernails can be hazardous to buttplay and can stop your fun just as you're getting started. With a little preparation, you can easily safeguard your body's most ultra-sensitive skin from an unnecessary OUCH—or worse. Be sure to cut nails short, and file until smooth, so there are no rough edges or hangnails.

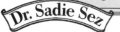

A secret to long fingernails and analplay

Did you know you don't have to sacrifice your long sexy fingernails to enjoy safe analplay? You can assign a DPF—Designated Play Finger. Simply clip and file the nail short on your chosen finger until it's smooth and analplay-ready. This will still leave you with nine long, luxurious fingernails—and one outrageous conversation starter!

Dr. Sadie Sez

Go carefree hair-free

Fur. It's cute on small animals—maybe not so much on your butt.

You've got several ways to remove nature's fur coat, if you so desire. Take yourself to a licensed salon specializing in intimate hair removal—or try doing it yourself:

♥ **SHAVING.** It's inexpensive and easy, but shaving can leave you with razor burn, itching and overnight stubble. For the best results, use a quality, multiple-blade razor with a swivel-head and shaving gel. For a quicker shave, trim with an electric shaver first. Start by wetting the skin and spreading the gel. Place one foot up on the bathtub edge to gain access between your cheeks and use your free hand to hold a cheek to the side. If you need more access, try squatting. Touch the blade lightly to the skin, and shave slowly with the grain, from the outer edge of the A-spot, on out. Feel for remaining hair tips, then shave in an upward, then downward stroke for baby-soft smoothness. When finished, rinse, pat dry with a soft towel, and apply a dusting of baby powder or special intimate after-shave.

♥ **LASERING.** Performed by a licensed specialist, this pulsing-light hair removal technique is safe, effective, FDA-approved—and costly. Full smoothness takes several treatments, and you must return every few weeks after each batch of treated hair has fallen out.

♥ **WAXING.** This technique temporarily removes hair all the way down to the root, so you'll enjoy more hair-free time than from shaving, and without the annoying stubble. Performed by a licensed specialist, she will spread a layer of hot wax on the butt cheeks and in the butt cleavage. She'll then place a cloth on top and rip it off with a quick motion—taking the wax, the hair and a little piece of your sanity. While some people find it too painful, others say it's a small price to pay for a smooth, sexy butt.

♥ **ELECTROLYSIS.** While this is the only permanent 100 percent guaranteed technique for hair removal—it's also the most painful. A certified specialist inserts a super-thin probe into each hair follicle, which sends a tiny electric current to zap the follicle, eliminating it forever.

Embarrassment's in the eye of the beholder

Both men and women can end up with butt-hair—and many don't care if they do. Your lover may not care, either. But if fur's not for you or your partner, there's no need to make love in the dark. Try one of the hair removal options in this chapter. Don't mind hair? Then just use extra lube to make everything super-slippery and minimize tugging and pulling.

Dr. Sadie Sez

5 Backdoor Anatomy Map

Isn't it amazing how the irresistible
attraction between men and
women comes from all
the ways our bodies
are *not* alike?

Vive la difference!

Until you get to the A-spot.

Here, you and your lover
are nearly identical—in form,
sensitivity and response. Think
of it as just one more thoughtful
sexual gift from Mother Nature.

37

But why is similarity a gift? Because now you can know exactly how it feels to receive the same intense pleasures you give. Who'd have ever thought your own backside could also be your guide to being a better lover?

Your similarities don't end at the A-spot, either. All but one of the deeper thrills are identical, too. But since you can't see your way to them, this simplified anatomy map shows you everything you need to visualize while pleasuring each other.

The backdoor anatomy map

Viewing these arousable areas on this anatomy map takes you only part of the way to ecstasy. Knowing how each one functions—along with how to pleasure them safely—takes you the rest of the way to fun, erotic, let's-do-it-again analplay.

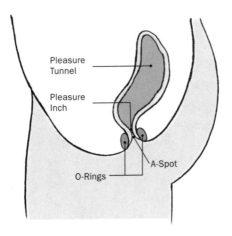

♥ **A-SPOT.** The *anus*—the entrance—is puckered at first, but capable of wide expansion with lots of warm-up and relaxation. It's made of soft tissue (similar to the thin delicate skin of your lips) that's densely packed with zillions of ultra-sensitive pleasure-receptive nerve endings that deliver those signature A-spot sensations.

♥ **O-RINGS.** The *sphincters*—circular muscles at the A-spot's entrance—come two to a lover. You can easily flex your outer O-ring at will, yet its tandem twin is set by nature on autopilot, meaning its control is completely involuntary when you go to the bathroom—one reason being relaxed is so essential to your enjoyment and safety.

♥ **PLEASURE INCH.** The *anal canal*—that first inch or so inside the A-spot—is a narrow passageway of soft sensitive tissue that, together with the O-rings, has an amazing ability to expand when relaxed. This 'squeeze of tightness' is a major pleasure center, for both giver and receiver.

♥ **PLEASURE TUNNEL.** The *rectum*—the six-to-nine inch tube beyond the Pleasure Inch—is a gentle 'S' curve of looser folds of soft, smooth tissue which can expand during arousal to accept a penis or sextoy.

Your backdoor anatomy sensors

Even subtle changes in the way you touch your lover's backside can mean the difference between *"ouch"* and *"ohhhhh!"* Be a savvy lover by understanding how each area responds best to different stimulation:

♥ **TOUCH.** The A-spot and Pleasure Inch—your lover's most sensitive areas—usually respond to light touching, sweet caressing and subtle vibration.

♥ **PRESSURE.** As you glide into the Pleasure Tunnel, your lover's pleasure receptors are more pressure-sensitive—and can respond favorably to feelings of fullness that come with penetration.

BYO slippery stuff—here's why

There's a good reason you don't see any lubrication glands on the anatomy map—*there aren't any*. This means the only way to slide is to provide your own glide, by using water-based or silicone lube. You'll not only awaken every one of those pleasure receptors, you'll avoid injuring the thin and sensitive tissue, which keeps your experience safer, more comfortable and more pleasurable.

What the A-spot is not

At first glance, you may find the next sentence to be totally obvious:

The A-spot is not a vagina.

Yet it's worth saying, because in the heat of the moment, it's easy to forget. And if you ever treat it like a vagina—without the necessary preheating, relaxing and lubing—you're heading down the wrong path.

The exotic way men and women differ inside

You and your lover each have an explosive orgasm spot a few inches inside the A-spot. And while they're both in the same general area—the way you stimulate them, the way they arouse and the orgasms they can produce—are different for each of you.

The female pleasure trigger is called the G-spot. The male orgasm trigger is the He-spot. Each is accessible from inside the A-spot, and each can deliver powerful orgasms. So why aren't they on this map? Because they're waiting for you in Chapter 10.

Before you touch, get **IN** touch

How'd you like to learn a lot more about yourself AND be rewarded with intensely satisfying orgasms? When the coast is clear, bring a hand-mirror into bed with your naked self—and come meet your own A-spot. Admire its starfish beauty. Watch how it flexes when you gently touch it. Feel the joy when you run a lubed fingertip around its rim. Pretty exciting, yes?

Dr. Sadie Sez

6 Sensual Booty Massage

Like everyone else, you probably take your backside for granted. Yet you rely on these muscles all day long for standing, walking, climbing and running. They even save you from passing gas in crowded elevators.

No wonder your butt's always tired, achy and tight!

But how often do you think about turning it into a playing field of pleasure—not just to soothe your lover's aching muscles, but to excite that soft receptive skin? As an often overlooked erogenous zone, those two cheeks are always eager for sensual arousal from kneading, squeezing, kissing, licking, spanking, gentle biting, feather-light touching—or simply calming moments of warm-handed stillness.

Why stop at the cheeks? Lustily arousing the hips, waist, small of the back, inner thighs and A-spot can add thrilling new dimensions to your lovemaking.

What's a good massage without special touches?

♥ **SET THE MOOD.** Start by creating a warm, cozy environment: Low lighting, soft music, a sexy aroma, and a warm air temperature that's comfortable for naked bodies, which helps you calm down, heat up—and open up.

♥ **WARM THE DIGITS.** Ice-cold hands? Heat them under hot running water, or simply nestle them between your own thighs before touching your lover's skin. Pre-warmed massage oil can add a nice sensation as it heats up your touch.

♥ **GET SLIPPERY.** No massage is complete without slick hands gliding across frictionless skin. Choose a high-quality massage oil—or if you're planning on slipping your fingers inside—use a silicone lube for your sensual massage.

♥ **POSITION YOURSELF.** Are you comfortable? If not, you'll be crampy and tired and done before you know it. Assume a comfortable position that also lets you leverage your body weight to minimize or maximize pressure.

♥ **MIX IN THE EXTRAS.** Playfully tease your lover with a feather tickler, or deliver an erotic surprise with a petite spanking paddle. Wear your hair long? Sweep it lightly up and down and all around your lover's naked booty. Haven't shaved in a few days? Tease her gently with your facial scruff.

♥ **INVITE FEEDBACK.** Harder? Softer? Higher? Lower? It's okay to ask. You may even be surprised how much pressure your lover enjoys.

♥ **LISTEN UP.** Stay alert for signs your magic is working: deep sighing, budding goosebumps, involuntary shivers, warming skin—or a long, deep, passionate kiss.

Blushing Cheeks

Cup one palm onto each cheek, and rub slowly in circular motions until the skin warms to the touch. Try kneading and squeezing, too. Now form soft fists, and slowly twist them into the center of your lover's cheeks.

Pray For More

Bring the flats of your hands together, with your pinkies at the top of your lover's butt cleavage. Begin sliding the sides of your pinkies on a long, slow ride down, nestling them in for maximum pleasure. Now glide them back up, and repeat slowly, over and over. What if you were to add in a subtle wavelike motion?

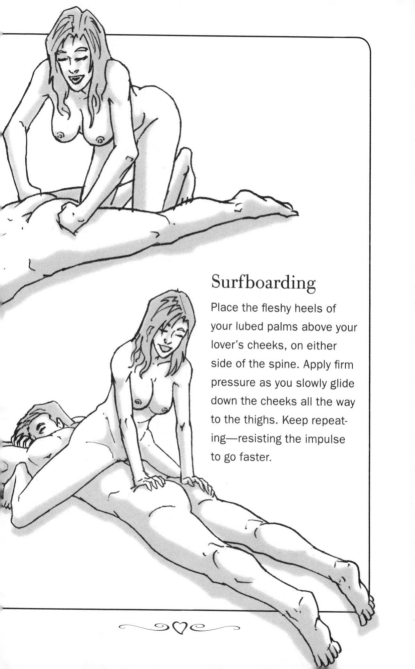

Surfboarding

Place the fleshy heels of your lubed palms above your lover's cheeks, on either side of the spine. Apply firm pressure as you slowly glide down the cheeks all the way to the thighs. Keep repeating—resisting the impulse to go faster.

Crease Rider

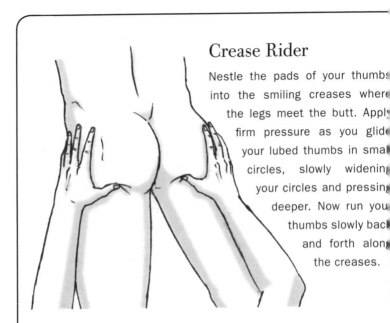

Nestle the pads of your thumbs into the smiling creases where the legs meet the butt. Apply firm pressure as you glide your lubed thumbs in small circles, slowly widening your circles and pressing deeper. Now run your thumbs slowly back and forth along the creases.

Coochie care

Getting slippery can sure get sloppy. But every woman has to be careful to keep massage oil that's touched the A-spot from trickling down to the vagina, since this oil can carry bacteria. I recommend this: While she's on her tummy, roll-up a small hand towel, and nestle it between her legs, against her taint. This barrier should absorb any runoff, so you can go ahead and get slippery-sloppy!

Taint Treat

Spread open your lover's legs, and place your lubed fingertips onto your lover's taint. Slowly, gently, move your fingertips in small circles, applying only light pressure, as you advance from sensual massage to sexual pleasure. (Note to women: slightly firmer pressure can begin indirectly stimulating his orgasm trigger—the He-spot!)

All Thumbs

Gently place both thumbs deep between your lover's cheeks, on either side of the A-spot. Use soft pressure as you slowly glide your thumb-pads up and out to the sides. Now repeat as you move your thumbs down slightly each time, until you reach the taint. Now start at the top again.

Modesty OFF— Direct A-spot massage ON!

The pleasure of direct A-spot massage is more than how good it feels. It also comes with your lover's promise that it's all about caressing the *outer* A-spot—nothing deeper. This helps relax new-comers, as well as reassure lovers who've agreed to keep buttplay on the mild side.

Thumb Roller

Gently place one lubed thumbpad onto the A-spot, then stroke down and lift—just as the thumbpad from your other hand follows right behind. Continue twiddling, one thumb after the other, as your lover's A-spot craves each sensual contact more and more.

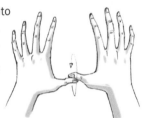

Butt Buffer

With one lubed fingerpad touching your lover's A-spot, slowly glide it back and forth, like a slow-mo windshield wiper—in full and glorious contact with that hot puckering spot.

7 Fingerplay

What if you discovered a secret seduction spot on your lover?

What if your lover found that very same spot on you?

What if you started playing around with each other's spots?

What if you both *l-o-v-e-d* playing with these spots and now can't keep your hands off each other?

That, dear friend, is how you put the *us* in *anus!*

Finding your own fingerplay comfort level

Your lover's "secret seduction spot" is the totally arouse-able A-spot, of course. But what if you're feeling uneasy about having your *own* spot touched?

Try this. Next time you're deep into the excitement of foreplay, instead of giving your lover a knee-jerk "no" or a modest "maybe"—give yourself permission to feel a few moments of your partner's gentle, loving fingertip touch. You might be pleasantly surprised. After all, your partner is simply pleasuring another of your erotic epicenters.

Still not for you? That's perfectly okay.

Totally for you? Congratulations! You've added a passionate new dimension to foreplay—and perhaps the start of something much more....

Learn your lover's silent language of love

Without a word, your partner is always telling you whether pleasure is growing—or slowing. This silent posturing is known as body language, and if you're uncertain how to interpret it, it's okay to ask thoughtful questions, such as: "Would slower feel better?" or "Are you ready to go a little deeper?" or "Do we need a little more lube?"

Share the intense joy of less

The moment your finger first touches the A-spot should thrill your lover to the core. But do you know how to electrify that moment in a way that sets off bursts of sexual fireworks that will rocket your lover to the moon?

Do nothing.

That's right: hold still. But remember that doing nothing doesn't mean your lover is feeling nothing. *Au contraire!* The A-spot is so sensitive, your stillness can set off a chain reaction of pulsing, quivering sexual excitement—no matter which level of fingerplay you're enjoying.

THE **5** LEVELS OF
Fingerplay

Fingerplay can be as subtle—or surreal—as your lover desires. And it's up to you two to find the comfort levels that suit your sexual appetites.

The good news is you have five levels of fingerplay to choose from, and each of you is perfectly free to choose your own level. So go ahead—be as wild or mild as you like.

LEVEL I
Finger*padding:*
No-penetration fingertip fun

Even if you're a bit squeamish, giving fingerpad is no big deal. But *getting* fingerpad can trigger waves of pleasure that ripple throughout your lover's sensual nervous system—as long as you remember one all-important rule-of-thumb: touch gently.

This is the way you switch on the zillions of ultra-sensitive pleasure receptors packed into your lover's A-spot. What's more, these thrills aren't even the main course—they're more of a side dish to your lovemaking already in progress.

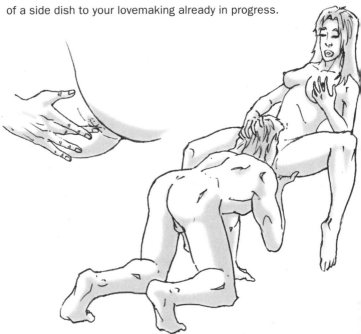

Remember: like a love note to the A-spot, the lubed finger never goes in—it just teases and pleases at the entrance, like this:

Pat

Gently tap the center until you drive your lover crazy. Vary your speed. Feel a subtle suction each time you lift off.

Pet

Glide your fingerpad over the A-spot repeatedly in a sensual "come-hither" motion, or slowly spell out a saucy love message, letter by letter.

Cuddle

Nestle your fingerpad into the A-spot with soft pressure—and hold still. Tactile thrills for your lover, mental thrills for you.

Shimmy

How subtly can you twitch your fingerpad? If it's like the small quick movements of a shiver—you've got it. Now try it!

Orbit

Gently glide your slippery fingerpad s-l-o-w-l-y around the rim, like you're circling Uranus! Go clockwise—then try counter-clockwise.

LEVEL 2
Finger*tipping:*
Mild penetration with wild sensation

If you were over-the-moon with fingerpadding, perhaps just an inch of subtly slim penetration is in your future. That's the joy of fingertipping: going in just a little—to the smaller first knuckle—and no further.

The secret to giving good fingertip? Warm up with great finger*pad*—then at the right moment, with light pressure, a little lube and a willing lover, gently slip your fingertip inside.

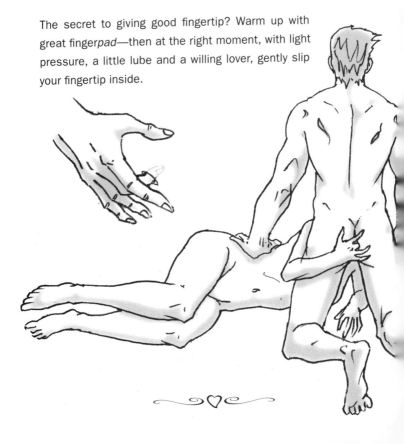

Slide inside only about an inch—to that very first knuckle—then hold still to let your lover revel in wild sensations and intense pulsations. Then resume your magic. Remember—*tiny* motions create *big effects*:

Plug

Slip your fingertip inside only as far as the first knuckle—then hold perfectly still as you give oral love. Can you feel the hot quivering?

Flutter

With the subtlety of a low tremor, wiggle your finger at the knuckle.

Circle

Move in tiny circular motions with your fingertip. No hula-hooping, please.

Probe

Ever so s-l-o-w-l-y, glide your fingertip in and out, never going further than the first knuckle each time you re-enter. Need to re-lube?

Synergy melts shyness

Fingerplay by itself can be heavenly. So can oral love-making, of course. If you've never combined the two, you're in for an extraordinary rush of excitement as the two simultaneous stimulations can build on each other to create exquisite pleasures and orgasms like you've never experienced. If your lover is a reluctant fingerplayer, try it while you're giving oral, when the heat of the moment can ease the hesitation.

Dr. Sadie Sez

LEVEL 3
Finger*pleasing:*
The sensual joyride of a full finger

Are you ready to experience the disappearing finger trick? You needn't be a magician, but the feeling is certainly magical.

If you enjoyed fingertipping, and felt your lover (or yourself) pushing back on that finger—gyrating, moaning, pulsating, and generally craving more than a slippery inch—perhaps you'll want to explore the fun of an entire finger.

The rules don't change during fingerpleasing. Minimal motion and stillness are still the mark of a masterpiece. And then it's up to you to sense how much your lover desires in-and-out pleasing.

Relax your finger and follow the natural contours and curves of your lover's Pleasure Tunnel. The slipperiness of lube makes everything come together beautifully. And an oral complement can be truly orgasmic!

Remember: after warm-up, gently insert your well-lubed finger—and never EVER flick. Then try these:

Corkscrew You

Hold your finger still and feel the hot pulsations. Slowly glide out, then fully back in again. Now use your wrist to revolve your finger during in-and-out stroking.

Knuckle Play

Press the big knuckle at the base of your finger into full contact with the A-spot's surface and keep it there. Now rotate your wrist in small circles, or rock back and forth as you apply constant, gentle, heavenly pressure to the A-spot.

Come-Hither

With your fingerpad facing your lover's tummy from the inside, gently stroke in a slow "come-hither" motion, massaging your lover's G- or He-spot. (More on these pleasure spots in Chapter 10.)

Rock Steady

Hold still and let your lover rock back and forth into your finger, giving over control of depth, speed and pressure. (Try placing your elbow against your own hip, so your body can leverage your lover's thrusting.)

LEVEL 4
Twin fingerplay = Twice the pleasure

If one finger feels extraordinary to you, will two fingers double your pleasure? For some, the answer is a very orgasmic YES!

Just remember: slower motions with extra lube are the keys to success—starting with these two different techniques for smoothly inserting the second finger:

Piggyback

With your lubed middle finger already comfortably inside, slide it *almost* all the way out. Now tuck your lubed index finger above or below the middle finger to create a tapered effect, then slide them slowly inside together.

Two-handed Teepee

Interlock all fingers of both hands and then extend both index fingers. Now slide one index finger down the other about half an inch, and slowly insert the lead fingertip, letting the second fingertip simply follow it inside.

LEVEL 5
Ninja fingers: For advanced lovemaking

Many lovers never go this far—while other lovers won't go without. What about you? It's perfectly okay to turn it away—or turn it up. Do you dare?

Just remember: make sure your lover's A-spot and all fingers stay coated with plenty of lube for the entire wild ride:

Freddy Flintstone

With your index and middle finger together inside, gently "run" them in place to create a uniquely rhythmic sensation.

Scoop du Jour

Slowly swipe your finger around the sides in half circles, like you're eagerly scooping the very last of the handcream from the jar.

Tug of Love

Gently curl your finger into a soft question mark. Now tug and twist ever-so-gently for a sensual soul-melting sensation.

Rockin' the Teepee

Using the Two-handed Teepee insertion technique, glide your well-lubed index fingers back and forth past each other for a real thrill.

Moon Probe

While both her hands are freed for playful mischief, he lies back and soaks in the satisfaction. Comfort and eye contact for all!

Hitchhiker

With your lover on all fours, slowly insert your lubed thumb into the A-spot as you excite her genitals with your other hand. The thumb's thickness can feel quite exhilarating.

8 Lick-O-Lingus!

Hey! Is that a sextoy in your mouth—or are you just happy to see me?

Yes—your tongue. And as long as you're already enjoying using it to eat, speak, taste and kiss (or impolitely express yourself!), here's one more highly sensual pleasure you can add to your sexual repertoire.

But first, let's explore what could easily be the world's most perfect sextoy.

Your tongue's muscles are arranged to give you precision control over motion, pressure, curl and flutter. The surface is textured silky soft. The feeling is slippery wet. The sensation is body-temperature hot. And the shape is tipped to tease.

What's more, with the right type of stimulation, your tongue is wired to trigger the release of pleasure hormones and euphoric neurotransmitters throughout your body—which means feelings of pure joy—whether you're eating or kissing or rimming.

Masterful A-spot seduction

By design, your lover's A-spot is closed, tucked away, and not keen on sneak attacks. Your erotic mission: Warm it, seduce it, tease it—so the moment your tongue-tip touches it—arousal will be surging, resistance will be futile, and you'll be welcomed as a liberator.

Remember: the magic is in the journey—so don't rush. The more you tease, the more it craves. The stronger the build-up, the wilder the climax.

Rimming is its name. Pleasure is its game

Rimming—also known as a rim-job, tossing the salad, or the formal *analingus*—is the loving act of caressing and arousing the A-spot with the tongue and lips.

An acquired taste? Sure. Yet many say rimming is one of the most highly erotic, deeply personal and mentally thrilling expressions of physical pleasure ever—whether you're the lickee or licker. It's a lusty lovefest that comes with its own special feelings of vulnerability, bravery, conquest, creativity and passion.

And it arouses like nothing else—especially when you know the ins and outs.

Gassy? Maybe not so classy

Is tonight the night? Then tonight's not the night for internal combustion. While skipping gas-producing foods like beans, broccoli and milk during the day can help—it's no guarantee. Feeling a rumbling pressure building down there? Politely excuse yourself and let it out in another room.

Dr. Sadie Sez

Appetizers: Playful licking tips

When it comes to partner-pleasing, you can be timid or you can be creative. It's a good bet your lover wants the latter. Just start off gentle, then let yourself be:

♥ **LIPFUL.** No tongue, all lips—big and pouty and wet.

♥ **TUNEFUL.** Hum in different octaves until it's tickling just right.

♥ **FRENCHFUL.** Deep kiss like you're making out.

♥ **ZESTFUL.** Show curiosity and caress every centimeter.

♥ **CARNALFUL.** Become voracious and wild.

Don't just lie there— moan something!

Your lover is down there trying to excite you, hoping for a clue about whether or not the magic is working. Does it feel good? Then moan, purr, whisper or shout out how it feels! Silence is not golden.

Side dishes: Tempting tongue tips

Knowing *when* to tongue your lover's erotic center takes a sixth sense. Knowing *how* to tongue your lover's erotic center starts with these six skills:

Tap

Point your tongue-tip right at the center and send your lover a message in Morse code.

Swipe

Run the side of your tongue slowly along the A-spot for a long luxurious sensation.

Lap

Take long, luxurious licks, like you're devouring a melting ice cream cone.

Swirl

Lightly swirl around the outer edge, then spiral in. Relax so your tongue is floppy, not stiff.

Spell

Run the tip of your tongue through the alphabet, or spell out a secret fantasy. Be sure to dot your 'i's and cross your 't's!

Rub

Using the powerful muscles mid-way back on your tongue, press and rub its thick, broad surface into your lover's erotic center.

Main course: Tongue-a-liciousness!

As you grow more comfortable with each other, inhibitions often evaporate, and you may soon find yourself riffing like a jazz master. Try these grooves to keep you movin':

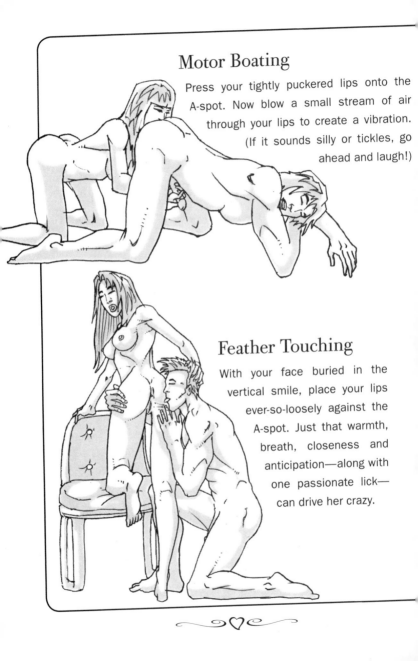

Motor Boating

Press your tightly puckered lips onto the A-spot. Now blow a small stream of air through your lips to create a vibration. (If it sounds silly or tickles, go ahead and laugh!)

Feather Touching

With your face buried in the vertical smile, place your lips ever-so-loosely against the A-spot. Just that warmth, breath, closeness and anticipation—along with one passionate lick— can drive her crazy.

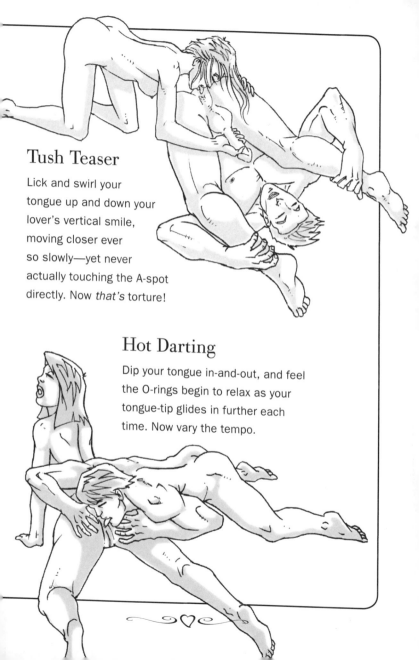

Tush Teaser

Lick and swirl your tongue up and down your lover's vertical smile, moving closer ever so slowly—yet never actually touching the A-spot directly. Now *that's* torture!

Hot Darting

Dip your tongue in-and-out, and feel the O-rings begin to relax as your tongue-tip glides in further each time. Now vary the tempo.

9 The Art of Penetration

Yes, anal penetration is an art.

Done right, it can create exhilarating pleasures, breath-taking sensations, and a heightened physical and emotional bond between you and your lover.

Done wrong, it can be uncomfortable—and unsafe.

The decision to partake is entirely up to you and your lover. And if that vote is a unanimous yes (even if it's only for someone's birthday!), here you'll find many intimate secrets to creating your own artistic masterpiece.

Success starts with passionate preheating

Whatever you choose for a grand entrance—excited penis or slippery sextoy—gliding in past the A-spot takes a special kind of foreplay. This erotic buildup includes open communication, trust, patience, care, a liberal slathering of lube and sexual stimulation—plus all this:

♥ **COOL YOUR HEELS.** Relax in a bubble bath. Sip fine wine. Meditate. Nap. Tune out the world. Tune into yourself. Be in the moment.

♥ **SET THE AMBIANCE.** Turn off ringers. Light scented candles. Cue some sexy music. Warm the room. And be sure condoms, wipes and lube are at hand.

♥ **CONNECT AND PLAY.** Kiss deeply. Massage that booty. Enjoy oral loving. Tease with light fingerplay. Plunge into vaginal intercourse. Just resist entering the backdoor as you keep your arousal rising.

♥ **COME AND GROW.** A first orgasm (or two!) can launch a woman from preheat to red hot, sending warm blood rushing into the entire pleasure zone—priming it with an inviting plumpness for the Main Event.

Making Your Grand Entrance

A Cheat Sheet by Dr. Sadie

✓ **Go slippery.** Lube up generously. Then re-re-re-lube.

✓ **Go slowly.** There's no rush. And pre-pre-pre-heat.

✓ **Go gently.** Choose positions that create the best angle and greatest comfort—especially for the receiver.

✓ **Go easy.** Never think of porn as your guide—it's a visual medium, where action is king. Instead, be slow and gentle.

✓ **Be open.** Your lover may be too new at this to give you enough verbal guidance—so ask.

✓ **Be safe.** The instant the penis touches the A-spot, it's off-limits for the vagina and mouth until it's thoroughly washed.

✓ **Be considerate.** The one receiving is in charge of how deep and fast you go—no forgetting the receiver's needs in the heat of the moment.

Ready for the glide inside?

If you've passed preheat and you're both piping hot, now's the moment: bring your two hot bodies together, place the head of the lubed, excited penis gently onto the A-spot—and start gliding the tip around the rim, teasing the A-spot to open. Let the receiver revel in the new and exciting sensations, as it teases you both about the pleasures to come.

Because the A-spot is snugger than the vagina, you may need to push a little more to send it inside—so aim counts! See which of these techniques are your favorites to guide 'n glide:

Guided Missile

He reaches down and holds the head of his erect penis directly against her A-spot—and guides himself in.

Good Doggy

While in the Doggystyle position, he holds the head of his penis steady against her A-spot—and she backs slowly onto it.

Sexy Assistant

She reaches around and holds the head of his penis against her A-spot—and guides him in.

Thumb Assist

He places the pad of his thumb right on the A-spot for aim, then does a quick switcheroo with his penis, and gently thrusts in.

The pleasures of receiving

Being the receiver comes with just as many erotic pleasures as the giver gets, and you'll enjoy them a lot more at the moment of penetration by remembering this:

♥ **GENTLY PUSH OUT.** It seems the opposite of what instinct would tell you, but gently pushing *out* at the same time your lover gently pushes *in* relaxes the O-ring muscles, and makes it more comfortable to receive.

♥ **BREATHE DEEPLY.** Breathing deeply is important, because it will relax your mind, your body and your A-spot. Before the moment of receiving, take three deep, long breaths. Then let out a long exhale as your lover enters.

♥ **SPEAK UP.** This is no time to be shy. Whisper (or moan!) your desires. Say "slower" or "faster" or even "hold still!" so *you* can control the thrusting. Ask for more lube. Let your lover know if something doesn't feel right.

What about the ol' switcheroo?

Did you notice I've only used the word "penis" as the penetrator in this chapter? This would seem to imply he's doing all the giving. But what if she's planning to wear a strap-on? Simply swap in "dildo" and turn to Chapter 12 for a little bit of erotic table-turning!

Dr. Sadie Sez

Skyrocket your deepest excitement

Once full penetration is achieved, you can start adding moves that'll lift you up that stairway to heaven. Try one or all of these exciters, so you can discover what you both may like:

Tip Dip

Glide the head just past the Pleasure Inch, then glide back out—never deeper—over and over. (Watch out...this could easily give him a fast-gasm!)

Love Yourself

If you're receiving, what are you doing with your *own* hands? Bring yourself to orgasm while receiving penetration and you may just see stars.

Eye Candy

Spread open your lover's butt cheeks and behold this visually erotic picture. But thrust slowly—since this can permit sudden deeper penetration.

Full Throttle

Is simultaneously filling both A-spot and vagina a fantasy of yours? To easily achieve your double-penetration fantasy (*without* another guy in the room!), learn about your sextoy options in Chapter 11.

Wiggle Room

As he holds perfectly still, she moves her hips all around to seek the angles and depth that tickle her fancy.

Roll 'n Rock

With penis inside and pelvis fully against her, gently gyrate or rock to tease the sensitive pleasure surface of her A-spot.

Ever hear the expression, "Hurts so good?"

In the heat of vigorous activity, the body can release a flood of pleasure hormones called "endorphins," which can actually transform feelings you'd think would be uncomfortable—into breathtaking sensations of pleasure and euphoria.

10 Orgasmic Spotplay

Can you *really* come from analplay?

And if you can, are there secret moves to help you get there?

And if you do, might it be as thrilling as you'd imagine?

The answers are *yes*, *yes*, and *yesssssssssss!*

Secret #1: Coming comes last

If you've breathlessly turned here seeking the key to coming during analplay, settle down. You're missing out on some real fun.

As many advanced lovers confide, much of buttplay's enjoyment comes from the extraordinary sensations you experience during lovemaking. In fact, it can actually *take away* from your pleasure when you're on a single-minded mission to capture the elusive A-spot orgasm.

Your best bet? *UN*-focus. Revel in the sensations of your lover's touch. Enjoy the many new and intimate discoveries about each other's bodies. Think of it as more of a journey than a destination.

Secret #2: Stay slippery

It's really no secret, because it's repeated throughout this book— and for good reason. Slathering on a good water- or silicone-based sex lube is absolutely essential for your pleasure, your safety, and perhaps even your orgasm.

Secret #3: Locate the trigger

You and your lover were each gifted with an orgasm trigger a few inches inside the A-spot. Locating it feels emotionally exciting. Touching it feels physically rewarding. And stroking it *just right* feels magnificent times ten.

But there's one rub: a man's orgasm trigger responds differently (and often more favorably!) than a woman's.

Which means your lover experiences this trigger's unique pleasures and orgasms differently than you.

And once you understand this basic physical difference, buttplay becomes even more of an intimate treat.

The G-spot: *Her* orgasm trigger

What does the orgasm spot you stimulate from within the vagina have to do with buttplay? Everything!

That spot is the Grafenberg spot, or more familiarly, the G-spot. This oval-ish area of spongy tissue about the size of a quarter is located two-to-three inches inside the vagina, on its upper wall. Visualizing it just behind the pubic hairline will help you find it more easily.

So how does it double as an orgasm trigger during analplay? Easy. Because the fleshy walls of tissue separating the vaginal canal from the rectal canal are so thin and supple, you may be able to stimulate the G-spot *with indirect pressure* from within the A-spot.

Every woman finds a different level of excitement from this indirect G-spot stimulation—from ho-hum all the way to OH-*MMMMMM*. And while your mileage may vary, it's worth exploring your full G-spot potential with your caring lover (or solo with a curved-tip sextoy!).

Guy's guide:
How to anally stimulate her G-spot

If it took you awhile to locate your lover's G-spot inside her vagina, you may wish there was a smartphone app to find it through her A-spot. Start here:

♥ After a thorough preheating of your lover's G-spot inside her vagina, slowly glide your re-lubed finger two or more inches inside her A-spot, aiming toward her belly button. Begin stroking the area in "come-hither" motions (assuming your fingers are long enough to reach), while lovingly asking her how it feels. Reminder: once your fingers touch the A-spot, there's no going back inside the vagina until those fingers are thoroughly washed.

Hey guys, how talented are you?

Wanna be a hero? Once she's thoroughly preheated, and lying on her back, slide two fingers inside her vagina. With your free hand also facing palm-up, glide one lubed finger inside her A-spot, choreographing a three-fingered "come hither" dance on her G-spot. And if she then places a vibrator on her clitoris, and a finger on her nipple, you may just be able to claim the prized four-erogenous-zones-at-once jackpot!

Dr. Sadie Sez

♥ When seeking the G-spot with your penis, position your bodies so the head of the penis presses into the G-spot. You'll find Doggystyle gives you an ideal angle, although you may find a new favorite in Chapter 13. And if you're using a dildo, your odds of success skyrocket if it's got a curved tip. Just aim for the G-spot, start thrusting slowly, and ask which moves feel good as you quicken your pace.

The He-spot: *His* orgasm trigger

Amazingly, guys have another powerful orgasm trigger besides the penis, yet many have never gone near it. A bit surprising, huh?

That spot is the prostate, which some call the "P-spot," and others (Tickle Kitty included) call the "He-spot." After all, it is about *him*. This walnut-sized gland is two-to-three inches inside the A-spot, just behind the pubic hairline. The prostate's job is to create and store much of the fluid for ejaculation, so millions of sperm can hitch a ride out of the body during orgasm.

Stroking the He-spot directly can actually trigger orgasms quickly and easily—even if the penis isn't being touched! Guys describe this type of orgasm as locally intense and mind-blowing (whereas women describe their G-spot orgasms as more full-bodied).

What holds so many guys back from experiencing this magnificent gift of pleasure? Penetration inhibition. Yet by exploring the techniques in this book with a caring, willing lover, he may discover an entire new world of sexual satisfaction awaiting at his own back door. And all you need is a single fingertip to get him there!

Gal's guide: How to stimulate his He-spot

Whether your guy is confident or cautious, giving him a He-spot orgasm can change his outlook on life—and on you. If he's game (all you have to do is ask!), here's what comes next:

♥ Always touch his He-spot with care. Remember, it's a gland. Start with light fingertip rubbing, using the same pressure you'd use to rub your eyeball through a closed eyelid. Try stroking the He-spot with either a "come hither" stroke or a windshield wiper motion (but no poking, please!).

♥ No matter how you're stroking him, he may not be able to discern your exact motions. Try two different stroking styles, and then whisper, "Do you like A...or B?" This will make it practical for him to guide you. From there, it gets easier by simply asking: Harder? Softer? Slower? Faster?

♥ Don't be surprised if he loses his erection—it's perfectly common—but you may need to reassure him as well. This doesn't mean he's not having the time of his life, or that he won't come—it's just his body's way of directing all his energy and focus to your loving touch as his pelvic and O-ring muscles relax. If you want to really blow his mind, blow him at the same time!

♥ If he does orgasm from prostate play, his ejaculate may flow out—rather than in his customary squirts or streams. Or he may show all the physical signs of coming, yet nothing comes out. Or he may never come this way at all. And guess what? It's all okay.

♥ If you're wearing a strap-on, find out more about it in Chapter 12, and review the penetration tips in Chapter 9. Then get ready for the time of his (and your) life!

Can a woman ejaculate, too? Yes, and proudly!

If you are blessed with being wired to orgasm from G-spot play, it just might include a real ejaculation! And while this usually scentless and colorless liquid will either flow, trickle or gush out of your urethra, I guarantee it's not pee. It's a "shejaculation". And not only is it perfectly normal, and feels heavenly, but I'll bet your lover finds it highly erotic!

Dr. Sadie Sez

Can You *Spot* The Differences?

It's not a contest, but there is a prize!

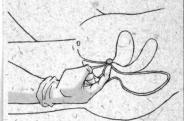 

Her G-spot	His He-spot
About 2-to-3 inches inside A-spot	About 2-to-3 inches inside A-spot
On upper vaginal wall, toward belly button	On upper anal wall, toward belly button
Stimulate-able with indirect pressure through rectal wall	Stimulate-able with direct pressure on gland on rectal wall
Chestnut-sized, bumpy texture, spongy	Walnut-sized, "palm-of-hand" texture, squishy
Grows larger & firmer during arousal	Grows larger & spongy during arousal
Initially responds to gentle-to-intense pressure	Initially responds to gentle pressure
Arouse with fingers, penis or curved-tip sextoy	Arouse with fingers or curved-tip sextoy
Responds to "come-hither" and "back 'n forth" stroking, plus tapping, circling, vibration	Responds to "come hither" and 'back 'n forth' stroking, plus tapping, circling, vibration
Pressure may cause "gotta pee" feeling	Pressure may cause "gotta pee" feeling
Even better with added clitoral stimulation	Even better with added penis stimulation
Not every woman can orgasm from it, even with clitoral stimulation	Many men orgasm from it, especially when combined with penis play
Highly satisfying, even without orgasm	Highly orgasmic, even without erection
Can produce powerful full-bodied orgasms	Can produce intense, localized orgasms
Orgasm may include "shejaculation"	Orgasm usually includes ejaculation

11 Hot Butt Toys

While you're reading this, teams of designers, engineers and sexperts around the globe are dreaming up new devices for the betterment of humankind: pleasuring the backdoor. You could spend a lifetime trying their many orgasmic creations.

But then you'd have a funny walk.

Instead, why not narrow your choices to a handful of exciting butt toys that'll thrill you the most? And with this chapter as your personal guide, you can get right to the bottom line.

Tour the Butt-toy Four

Toys designed for buttplay generally come in four clearly defined styles: *plugs, beads, prostate massagers* and *dildos.*

What makes these toys unique to buttplay? Aside from their anatomically tailored design, they all come with two important safety features: a tapered tip for easy insertion, and a flared safety-base to prevent them from ever completely disappearing inside.

This peace-of-mind design enables you to safely explore butt toys with your lover—or during passionate playtimes all by yourself. Your toy can serve as lovemaking's main course, or as a tasty side dish that accompanies rousing activities yet to come.

Either way, preheat before inserting your toy—and *always* slather plenty of lube over every inch of what's going inside.

Pleasure options, you ask?

Once you select your favorite toy styles, you can now explore a world of tush-tickling add-ons:

♥ **BUZZ.** Want to tune in to your own orgasmic frequency? Opt for variable-speed vibrations.

♥ **FEEL.** Would a soft, sensual lifelike material thrill your sensitive A-spot, or would a smooth and firm sensation quicken your pulse?

♥ **GIRTH.** Would slipping in a slim-shaped toy feel best, or ease fears? Or would "hurts-so-good" thickness be the eye-opening joyride you seek?

♥ **COLOR.** Would a vivid red or swirl of purple add to your playfulness? Or might you be comfortable with a deep dark indigo to mask any potential organic color?

♥ **WATER-RESISTANCE.** Germ-phobic? Hop into the shower with a water-resistant butt toy and enjoy a self-rinsing ride.

♥ **SENSITIVITY.** Are allergies or latex reactions holding you back? Then choose hypoallergenic or latex-free toys for a reaction-free playtime.

Ladies: Here's my secret for putting an "O" in buttplay

While buttplay feels highly arousing, it may not lead you to the promised land. That's why I recommend you take matters into your own hands. While your lover is lustily exciting your A-spot, you can touch a mini-vibrator to your clitoris—just the way you like it—and magnify the intense analplay sensations with over-the-top clitoral pulsations. Promised land—here you come!

Dr. Sadie Sez

Plugs: Fulfillment like you've never felt

Glide it in—then leave it in!

That's the beauty of a plug. It's shaped to stay put—not slide in and out—delivering a satisfying feeling of fullness combined with highly erotic sensations. And since it stays in place by itself, your hands are free to roam and play.

If you're a newcomer, a plug is a great place to start. It'll help you get used to the sensations of relaxing, squeezing, probing and pulsing. It's tapered at the top for easy glide-in, wider in the middle for that lusty sensation of fullness, then narrow at the neck of the base, so your O-rings can wrap snugly around it. The flared base then keeps it from ever going fully inside—easing your mind to focus solely on pleasure.

Beads: Bliss with each orgasmic burst

What a simple design—what a powerful rush!

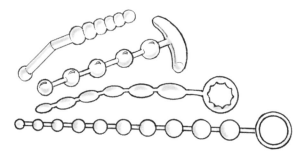

This entire toy is merely a strand of several smooth beads, spaced about half an inch apart, with a pull-ring safety-base on the end. You can choose all-the-same-size beads, or jazz it up with beads strung in different arrangements for a whopping mega-thrill when each bead slips out.

The pleasures begin as you gently slip each bead into your lover's A-spot—which delivers a thrill as it opens and closes the O-rings. Once the beads are all tucked away, leave 'em there to create pleasureful feelings of fullness and pressure as your other erotic activities bring orgasm closer and closer.

Then, at that divine instant your lover gets to that point of no return, slowly pull the strand straight out, one exciting bead at a time, so the A-spot opens and closes in delicious syncopation with those orgasmic pleasure bursts.

He-spot massagers: Precision on a mission

Boldly go where no orgasm has gone before.

By seeking out direct contact with the prostate, a He-spot massager can stimulate your guy to unexplored heights of pleasure. Your mileage may vary, yet it's almost always worth the ride.

A He-spot massager is cleverly designed with a gentle upturn at the tip for precision aim at the He-spot, as well as easy insertion. The toy's bulbous chassis is designed to feel good as it curves inside the Pleasure Tunnel. And its flared safety-base serves as a convenient joystick while it prevents the toy from slipping completely inside.

Start your adventure with plenty of preheating—never begin from a cold start. Lube up the toy, then insert it slowly into the A-spot, with the curved tip arching toward the belly button. If you've already found the He-spot with your finger, you'll find it a lot easier with the toy. Be sure to talk it through, so you'll know when there's direct contact. Then gently rub and massage directly on the delicate He-spot—never poke or prod. Or you can simply maintain a steady light pressure while turning your full attention to the art of penis pleasing.

Once you're comfortable with a basic He-spot massager, you can try hands-free models, which use natural muscle movements to excite the He-spot during lovemaking. And some designs even offer simultaneous taint stimulation for extra pleasure.

Once your guy gets comfortable with A-spot play, he'll discover a new world of pleasure—along with better control over his O-rings, pelvic muscles and orgasms. This can lead to a highly coveted new-and-improved prowess in bed.

Dildos: Probing for pleasure

Play it by hand—or slip one into a strap-on.

Either way, a dildo is designed with one goal in mind: to penetrate for pleasure. A dildo can be as small as a finger, or big as an arm. It can look sleek like a rocket, or real like an actual penis. It can be rigid and unyielding, or playful and bouncy. It can feel smooth and supple, or lifelike and rubbery. It can resemble an actual banana, or look like a wild animal. It can even come with bouncy balls, corkscrew ridges or flashy glitter.

It simply comes down to what you like.

But since all dildos are not designed specifically for analplay, your best bet is to choose one with a flared base, to give you a solid hand-or-harness grip, and to prevent it from ever disappearing completely inside. And if you're aiming for G- or He-spot fun, chose a dildo with a curved tip.

Be A Dildo Decider

What's your inner passion?

LENGTH

☐ Small & merciful

☐ Medium & magnificent

☐ Long & luxurious

GIRTH

☐ Narrow & nice

☐ Medium & manageable

☐ Wide & wicked

FEEL

☐ Smooth & silky

☐ Textured & bumpy

☐ Realistic & natural

FLEX

☐ Hard & rigid

☐ Bendy & bouncy

☐ Firm & giving

TIP

☐ Pointy & pleasing

☐ Medium & magical

☐ Stout & stupendous

EXTRAS

☐ Balls that bounce

☐ Bases with suction

☐ Upturn for G- or He-spot fun

If you're a thrill-seeker, try securing a standout suction-cup model dildo to the wall of your shower, and give new meaning to steamy. Or double your partner pleasure with a wild double dildo. You can even pump-up an inflatable dildo (or plug) to the girth and firmness that you call perfect! If you can imagine it, chances are they've already built it.

Your guide to toy safety

Toys are meant to be all fun and games—and they are—when you follow a few safety guidelines:

♥ **SMOOTH IT.** Feel around on new toys for any sharp edges or rough seams. File off any burrs until the toy is perfectly smooth. For ultimate smoothness, roll a condom over it.

♥ **CLEAN IT.** Wash toys thoroughly before and after each use with an adult toy cleaner or antibacterial soap—then rinse thoroughly and air dry. If there are batteries, be sure to remove them first.

♥ **STOW IT.** After cleaning and air drying, wrap each toy in its own clean cloth or fresh plastic storage bag, then store it in a cool place that's out of direct sunlight—and away from prying eyes.

♥ **COVER IT.** Certain toys have microscopic nooks and crannies that can harbor germs even if you clean those toys thoroughly. For the best protection, roll a condom over every toy—every time.

♥ **LUBE IT.** Always lube-up your toys—*but do not use silicone lube with a silicone toy.* It seems like the opposite of what you'd expect, but silicone-on-silicone will actually melt the toy. Instead, use a water-based lube with your silicone toy, or wrap it in a condom.

♥ **NEVER DO IT.** Do not insert bullet vibrators into the A-spot—unless you want to explain to the ER doc why it's lost inside your anus. Always use toys designed specifically for buttplay: models that are made with flared safety-bases to prevent them from disappearing inside.

12 Strap-on Seduction

Have you heard the one about the woman, the man, and the strap-on?

There are certainly plenty of groan-worthy jokes on this once taboo topic, yet these form-fitting harness/dildo combos are no joke at all—they're serious erotic devices that allow lovers to penetrate each other in new and exciting ways that were physically impossible before.

Worn by women (and increasingly by men!), a strap-on calls for an open-minded, open-cheeked partner willing to experience all the pleasures of being penetrated. Many lovers find it creates deeper intimacy and adds new levels of erotic excitement to their sexual repertoire. In your secret fantasies, could this be you? Or your lover? Or *both* of you?

Then read on! You'll not only find out about the types of harnesses and fittings available today—you'll learn how to choose one with a fit and feel that's as natural as an extension of your own body.

And that's when your *real* fun begins....

What's a strap-on anyway?

Today's term "strap-on" serves as convenient shorthand for a pair of items that together creates physical and emotional pleasures during oral, anal or vaginal penetration.

A strap-on *harness* fits snuggly around the wearer, most often at the waist. A strap-on *dildo* has a flat, flared base to steady it in position once you slide it through the opening on the front of the harness.

Choosing the right harness/dildo combo comes down to what fits best, feels right, suits your mood, and arouses your excitement. Where do you start? Right here:

♥ **CHOOSE YOUR FEEL.** Harnesses come in an array of natural and synthetic fabrics, such as leather, vinyl, rubber, nylon, plastic, spandex and polyester.

♥ **MATCH YOUR MOOD.** Be cute with polka dots. Go sassy with pink or purple leather. Or try sexy, red-hot vinyl, sleek black leather or fetish-ready rubber. Or choose a harness adorned with a shiny sheriff's badge to give you a feeling of swagger and authority!

♥ **MATE YOUR HARNESS AND DILDO.** Some harnesses make this choice easy, because they're designed for just one size dildo—while other harnesses come with nifty snaps to change retaining ring sizes—allowing it to support dildos of greater and greater girths.

♥ **TRY ON YOUR STRAP-ON.** Many sex shops encourage you to try on the harnesses you're considering—but *over* your pants, please! You'll know you've found the right fit when it feels comfortable and snug enough for confident motion and thrusting—with minimal sliding and no skin-pinching. Make sure the harness positions the dildo right on—or just above— your rock-solid pubic bone.

∽∾♡∽∾

♥ **ADD IN YOUR BONUS THRILLS.** Look for models with a secret bullet vibrator pocket to deliver direct clitoral stimulation. Or try textured bumps that will rub your clitoris the right way, either from inside the harness, or from the back of the dildo's flared base. You can even find harnesses with a plug (or two!) designed to penetrate the wearer.

Which harness will feel best on you?

With all these styles to choose from—come find the one that'll have you looking your sexiest, with the fit that hugs you best:

♥ **TWO-STRAP.** When you picture a strap-on, this is the style that usually comes to mind. Shaped remarkably like a 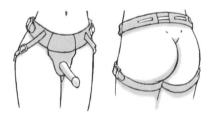 jockstrap, it's got one big difference: a hole in the center for your dildo. Many women like this model's snug fit, which allows more confident thrusting. And the two-strap not only braces the dildo firmly up against the woman's pubic bone—it leaves her labia, clitoris and vagina fully accessible for easy teasing 'n pleasing.

♥ **THONG.** Designed like a thong panty, this model straps on around the waist and straight up her vertical smile. Many women love how the strap automatically stimulates the clitoris during thrusting and penetrating. What's more, you can easily adapt the thong for all sorts of fun specialty attachments, including the couple-pleasing double dildo.

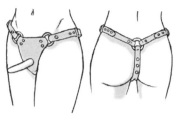

♥ **BIKING SHORTS.** Designed like a pair of stylish athletic shorts, this tight-fitting strap-on also offers post-sex practicality: simply toss it into the washer and dryer when you're finished. And while its design limits direct stimulation of the clitoris and vulva during playtime, it does give you a triumphant feeling like you've just won a bike-a-thon!

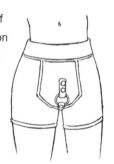

Swamped by strap-ons? Let me rescue you

I know too many choices can be overwhelming. If that's how you're feeling, you can bypass the a la carte section and head straight for the readymade kits. No guesswork—everything's already designed to fit together beautifully. And the kits won't cost you an arm and a leg—just think of it as your own personal stimulus package for being bold and brave.

Dr. Sadie Sez

♥ **DOUBLE PENETRATOR.** Ready guys? This one's for you to wear! In addition to holding almost any size dildo you like, it also comes with a generous opening to display your own proud penis. Why? So you can enter your woman through her vagina and A-spot simultaneously—like a ménage à trois (only with just the deux of you!). Or, if erections aren't always as on-demand as you'd hope, you're still guaranteed a strap-on hard-on that'll last all night long.

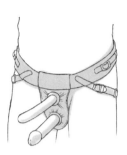

♥ **EVERYWHERE BUT THE TORSO.** If you can wrap it, you can strap it! These highly inventive strap-ons are designed for some wildly kinky places—like your chin, forehead, hand, chest or thigh. And if you think these strap-ons are only for the extra adventurous—think again. They're perfect for creating intense sexual satisfaction among the disabled as well as the voluptuous.

Going in for his thrill

When a woman is ready to experience the power of giving—and her guy is up for the adventure of receiving—that's the moment equal opportunity truly comes to your bedroom.

This reversal of roles is called "pegging"—a newly minted term that describes the timeless act of a strap-on wearing female proudly penetrating her guy's A-spot. Is this for you? It's entirely up to the two of you, of course, but a lot more guys are saying yes than ever before.

After harness and dildo are comfortably secured around her hips, it's playtime:

💜 **BE A SHOW OFF.** Proudly display your strap-on hard-on. Jump on the bed, parade around the room, let him see you go *boingy-boingy* with it. Feel the power swap and revel in the excitement of role reversal—or simply share a few laughs!

💜 **PLAY NAUGHTY.** How many times have you been talked into giving oral? Here's your chance to turn the tables: Ask *him* to give *you* a slippery handjob or a five-star BJ!

♥ **START SLOWLY.** Warm him up with fingers and small butt toys and follow the safe penetration techniques in Chapter 9. Use plenty of lube, and be patient and gentle as you slowly glide in past his O-rings.

♥ **SPEAK UP—BOTH OF YOU.** If you're newcomers at this, he may not be able to provide you enough feedback, so don't be shy about asking how he's doing. Take the lead.

♥ **POSITION WISELY.** A good starter position is Doggystyle, because it gives him a sense of control as he pushes back into you at his own pace and pleasure. Or try Missionary if he prefers the physical or emotional comfort of lying on his back. Ready to explore other positions? Flip to Chapter 13.

♥ **PAUSE 'N PLAY.** Once you've worked your way inside—hold perfectly still—and place your hands on his body to judge how he's doing. Remember: stillness feels good.

♥ **BE OBSERVANT.** Pleasure him with in-and-out thrusting—then switch to deep gyrating and grinding. Make note of which he prefers and fine-tune your anal loving techniques.

♥ **REV IT UP.** Spank his butt. Stroke his penis. Pinch his nipples. Or watch him self-pleasure. Make your motions more than just about penetration.

♥ **QUICKIES ARE OKAY.** It's perfectly fine if he says "that's good" after just a few minutes. Success isn't measured in duration—it's measured in adventure, pleasure and trust.

Remember: strap-on play is more about the shared joy and experience than it is about steering toward an orgasm that may or may not come. Simply revel in your newfound sensations and mutual fun.

Who *you?* In a strap-on?? C'mon!

If you've never tried on a strap-on—or never thought you would—consider this: You may find the pure mental thrills of it all worth exploring. Have you ever wondered what it'd be like to walk around with a hard on? Brandish one in front of your lover? Feel the thrill of role reversal? Then why not strap one on just for the fun and fantasy? You don't even have to penetrate!

Dr. Sadie Sez

The Dominator

An awesome sense of power, an overpowering sense of domination and a mutual sense of pleasure— in an easy, comfortable position.

Bareback Rider

Like stacking a dildo and penis end-to-end, she aims for his He-spot from behind—he strokes to his heart's content from the front.

Winged Pleasure

When he drapes his legs over her hips, she's in perfect position for loving penetration. He's able to assist by pulling her into him with his legs while her hand is poised for orgasmic stroking.

13 Positions of Pleasure

Whether you're giving or receiving, you are now at the brink of buttplay's ultimate joyride—the most satisfying full-body, full-pleasure adventure you may ever experience.

If you and your lover are already unzipping—*hold on!* Take a few moments to explore these tips, lust over the illustrations, and choose who'll be the lucky first receiver. Or you can simply turn the other cheek, if one of you feels this takes passion a bit too far.

As they say, *different strokes for different folks* (although they probably didn't mean buttsex when they said it!).

What's your position on positions?

The good news is, there's no right or wrong position for analplay intercourse—the very best (as always) comes down to whatever satisfies you most. After all, when you factor in personal flexibility, comfort, experience level, body size and shape, and top it off with lusty likes and inner desires—and everything feels right—you'll know you've scored your jackpot!

Wipe the phantom urge

Rebooting your booty for two-way traffic may come with pleasures you've never experienced—and one you never expected. Although you're playing with the sensitive nerve endings in your butt for fun, your brain may think you've got to poop—even though you don't. So relax. Those phantom feelings should fade as you grow accustomed to the joys of buttplay.

Dr. Sadie Sez

How to receive with ease

After enjoying the gift of your lover's passionate preheating, your body should now be ready, willing and open—with penetration feeling comfortable, natural and exciting. Here's how to keep these good sensations going:

♥ **STAY RELAXED IN THE MOMENT.** Breathe deeply—and remember that being relaxed isn't the same as being passive. Clear your mind, revel in the excitement, feel passions rise.

♥ **GUIDE THE GLIDE INSIDE.** Even with plenty of preheating and lube, you can relax the O-rings even more by gently pushing *out,* as your lover gently pushes *in.* Find even more arousing tips for easing-in on page 74.

♥ **SPEAK UP IF SOMETHING DOESN'T FEEL RIGHT.** Your partner is a lover, not a mind reader. Voice your needs, both good and otherwise—even if you're customarily the quiet type.

♥ **LET YOUR DESIRES BE YOUR GUIDE.** Do you want to be "taken?" Go Doggystyle. Do you crave feeling in control? Hop on top. Want to start slowly and lovingly? Try Spooning.

♥ **LET YOUR PASSION GROW ORGANICALLY.** Once you feel your excitement accelerating, you'll delight in how potential pain receptors can automatically and instantaneously switch into pleasure receptors.

How to give with ease

For the woman, giving simply involves wearing her best-fitting, ever-hard strap-on. Yet for the man, he may sometimes find he's looking down at an uncooperative penis. This doesn't mean there isn't wild arousal—it may simply signal there's another issue at play. What can you do? Try any of these:

♥ **SLIP INSIDE SMOOTHLY.** You should never need to cram, so pull back for a moment. Did you fully warm-up your lover? Are you using enough of the right lube? Are there distractions coming from outside the bedroom—or inside your head? Take a short, loving break, and try again.

♥ **KNOW SHE'S OKAY.** Are her loud moans inspired by pleasure—or discomfort? Why guess? If you've followed this book's prescription, she shouldn't be feeling any pain. Simply ask how she's doing. This way, you both can be at ease.

♥ **FIND YOUR PLEASURE POSITION.** Consider positions that are the most comfortable, so you can focus entirely on your grand entry and lovemaking moves.

♥ **FOCUS ON WHAT TURNS YOU ON.** The more you worry, the tougher it gets. Break the worry cycle by focusing on what mentally excites you. Love eye candy? Try Doggystyle. Crave deep eye contact? Get into Missionary. Enjoy full-body contact? Embrace Spooning.

Ladies: Help for his erection direction

Ohohooaahh! Was that your gasp of pleasure...or pain? If your lover mistakenly takes your excited moaning the wrong way, it can quickly soft-boil his hard-on—especially if he's a sensitive guy. So tell him in a moment of passion how much you want it. You can also reassure him that if you're ever uncomfortable, you'll let him know. Now...was that so hard?

Dr. Sadie Sez

THE OFFICIAL
Tickle My Tush
POSITION GUIDE

Have fun exploring these exciting tried-and-true pleasure positions. Crave more? Pick up Dr. Sadie's bestseller, *Ride 'Em Cowgirl!—Sex Position Secrets for Better Bucking* and adapt the more than 100 positions into new backdoor adventures for both of you.

Missionary Possible

What you'll like: Greater body and eye contact, deeper penetration, and more comfort for muscles and joints. It also aligns you for passionate kissing, lusty access to breasts and orgasmic genital play. Ideal for lovers of different heights and weights, too.

X-tra Hot: The receiver draws knees to chest, which raises up the butt for deeper, sexier access.

Jelly Roll

With receiver's legs to one side, you can push and pull in erotic harmony. Try gently rocking on an extended downstroke, giving the receiver plenty of pleasure thrills while you both enjoy extraordinary body views and orgasmic genital play.

Wish Boner

With hands gripping ankles, you can now target the G-spot with shallow (but strategic) penetration. Heighten the excitement with a hands-free vibrator dancing on her clitoris. A well-positioned towel-covered pillow under the receiver's butt completes the magic.

Doggystyle

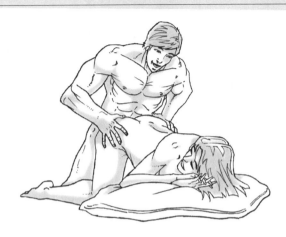

What you'll like: This come-from-behind victory is tailor-made for anal sex, because you can keep going and going. It's more than just comfortable for both of you—it allows you to maximize depth and power thrusting, as well as stimulate the vagina with fingers or toys at the same time.

X-tra Hot: With her head down and butt up, you've got the perfect position to zero-in on her G-spot, together with butt spanking, hair playing and back rubbing. Or reverse roles and go on a He-spot mission!

Red Cheeks

Ideal for positioning each other at the perfect height—his upright position lends itself to power thrusting, balance and leverage. Extra credit: can either of you imagine how this position gets its name?

Happy Crab

After a long hard day, the receiver can fully relax and enjoy a long hard night. The shallower penetration and ease of angling allows for glorious G-spot stimulation.

Ride 'Em Cowgirl!

What you'll like: Delivers exciting new angles with the woman in complete charge of depth, angle and pace. Offers access to breasts and clitoris (for both of you!), while his hands can assist her thighs to keep them from giving out. Plus, plenty of eye candy for him; exhibitionist fun for her.

X-tra Hot: If you're lucky enough to have a lover with a naturally upturned penis, you've got a living G-spot sextoy! Or choose her strap-on dildo with a gentle up-curve for a He-spot sensation.

Backfire

She enjoys the freedom to pump, just the way she loves it—in charge of speed, depth and G-spot angling. Features plenty of delicious eye-candy for him, and the potential for sexy spanking and cheek stroking. And it's ideal if he's large and she's petite.

View Master

Get outta the bedroom and into the chaise! What's his reward for having both hands free? He can push and pull her thighs and tease her clitoris as he drinks in the spectacular up-close eye-candy. And by all means, choose a stable chair!

Spooning

What you'll like: This warm, romantic position fosters feelings of intimacy while naturally minimizing depth. It reveals her neck and shoulders for kissing, her hips for hugging, and her breasts and clitoris for caressing. It also allows couples with height and weight differences to find a perfect fit.

X-tra Hot: If an expanding baby bump is making other positions impossible or uncomfortable, you've found your pleasure solution.

Bzzzzzzzzzz

Gaze deeply into each other's
eyes, as the vibration from her
hand-held vibrating egg
arouses her from the
front, and his rock-hard
penis arouses her from
behind. With her leg
aloft and steadied by
his impassioned grip,
this orgasmic pleasure is
indescribably delicious.

Full Spoon

Who says you can't
deep kiss during
intimate spooning?
Look deeply into
each other's eyes,
and feel completely
connected, as his
hands freely roam.

Finding yourself in a position pickle? Try these:

ANGLING TO PLEASE? Aiming for an elusive G- or He-spot? Try *pillows*—and lots of 'em! Use as many as you need to prop yourself where you want to be. You'll not only be more comfortable, you'll feel like you're making love on Cloud Nine.

ACHING BACK? Get off the bed. Try these easier-on-the-back positions. Sit on a couch or chair, so she can lower down onto you. Or stand beside the bed with your lover's butt beckoning you at the edge of the mattress. Or try a sex swing, sex sling or comfy sex positioning wedge.

HALF MAST? Even semi-hard can be a challenge up against a snug A-spot. If you still need a boost after trying eye-candy positions and manual stimulation, consider a pharmaceutical erection solution. With a doctor's okay, it'll ease your mind as you ease inside, with your virility and confidence in full display.

PART WAY? If you prefer receiving shallower thrusts, try Spooning. This allows you to keep your legs mostly closed during penetration, which stops him from penetrating too deeply. He can help out by holding your cheeks together, too.

SPEED RACER? Does your partner get so excited he always ends up pumping too fast—no matter what you say? Then change positions so *you're* on top. Now guess who's in charge?

BOUNTIFUL BOOTY? Is voluptuousness creating too much distance? Then bring all four of your hands to the rescue. While she curls on her side on the corner of the bed, he stands strategically beside her. Then she simply reaches behind to spread her own beautiful cheeks, so he can use his hands to aim and glide his penis right in.

CAUTION

UNPROTECTED SEX—EVEN ONCE—WHETHER ORAL, VAGINAL OR ANAL CAN POSE SERIOUS HEALTH RISKS TO YOU AND YOUR PARTNER. ALWAYS USE BARRIER PROTECTION AND FOLLOW THE SAFER SEX PRACTICES IN CHAPTER 3.

14

Frequently Assed Questions 2

Why does *Tickle My Tush*
provide a second FAQ in
the back? Because after
13 chapters of how-to advice,
several new and important
questions are bound to arise.

On behalf of your pleasure,
safety and confidence,
here you go.

Will everything return to normal tightness afterwards?

Yup! As long as you use lube and your lover doesn't use force. Over time, O-rings can actually gain flexibility, and accept penetration more easily. Just like most muscles in your body, they stretch— but don't *stay* stretched. Or else how could anyone ever walk normally after yoga?

Will analplay give me hemorrhoids?

It's unlikely. Hemorrhoids are normal veins in the A-spot and lower rectum that have become swollen, inflamed and very annoying. They're most often caused by straining to poop, or from added pressure during pregnancy.

Can I blame any gas afterwards on the dog?

Sure...but you better have a dog! In some cases, people do get gas, or even a tummy ache, from the pleasurable thrusting that can send air whooshing inside, especially in combo with any gassy or greasy foods recently consumed. Your best bet? On days you know that analplay is on the menu, keep the gaseous foods off your plate.

Will I still have full control over pooping?

If you use plenty of lube, and follow the recommendations in this book, you shouldn't become "accident prone." While only a few minor studies have been conducted on post-analplay incontinence, there are no conclusive results to report. In fact, some people say they've gained far *greater* muscle tone in their O-rings. Of course, for every rule of thumb, there are exceptions. And if you're having an issue, stop the analplay and consult a physician.

Why did I get so emotional from analplay?

Some people hold negative thoughts buried deep inside from a traumatic early toilet training and other negative messages directed "down there." Feeling this area probed for pleasure during adulthood can actually release this psychological baggage in a flood of unexpected negative emotions. If the gentle touch of a caring lover doesn't help you overcome these feelings on your own, please seek the help of a qualified psychological professional.

Am I okay with his ejaculate inside?

If you've both tested free of all STIs—and you've been 100% faithful— then yes, it's okay. What's more, unless any semen finds its way into the vagina, getting pregnant isn't a worry. Some of the semen will get absorbed into the body, and most will find its way out on the next trip to the bathroom.

AfterPlay

Do you know what says the most about your own sexual curiosity?

You're here right now, finishing this book.

And to you I say, *bravo!*

But no matter how deeply you embrace your curiosity and desire for orgasmic bliss, please remember—stay true to yourself by protecting your emotions and your body—each and every time you play.

It's my pleasure prescription for you, and it's worth filling.

X's and O's,

Dr. Sadie

Dr. Sadie

P.S. I'd love to hear how this book inspired you. Come talk to me: *facebook.com/doctorsadie*

Special Thanks!

To my all-star publishing team for another outstanding book: Editor J. Croker Norge, Illustrator Steve Lee, Book Designer Tom Klump, Cover Designer Alan Smithee, and my favorite tush-ticklin' sex coach, Reid Mihalko. You make me shine.

To all the adult novelty distributors, sextoy retailers, lingerie boutiques, home party entrepreneurs, bookstore owners, chain-store buyers and wholesalers, for helping to spread the education and fun as we satisfy our customers' sexual appetites.

To all the radio and TV shows, podcasts, magazines and news-papers bold enough to carry my message of sexual empowerment and liberation.

To all the original sex educators, counselors and therapists, for blazing the path to compassionate sex education for all.

To my supportive family, and especially Mom, for giving me the tools to survive and thrive. To my beautiful little girl, who brightens my life and makes me proud—every day. To my friends, who've stuck with me through thick and thin. To my special man and A., for your open hearts and unconditional love. And to the angel who lives on my shoulder, for keeping a close eye on me.

And to my readers and supporters—you—who've been with me over the past decade, and those who've written to share all the ways my advice has changed their lives for the better.

It's because of *you,* that I do what I do.

About the Author

When you need accurate answers about lovemaking, turn to Dr. Sadie Allison, founder and CEO of Tickle Kitty, Inc., as well as author and publisher of today's most popular line of fun, informative, how-to sex-help books.

As a leading authority on human sexuality for over a decade, Dr. Sadie's mission is to empower women and men to embrace a deeper enjoyment of their sexuality, through education, information and motivation. And with over two million copies of her sex-help books now in lovers' hands, her magic is working.

Since starting Tickle Kitty in 2001, she's grown her publishing house into a real powerhouse. From *Tickle His Pickle* to *TOYGASMS!*, *Ride 'Em Cowgirl!* and others, each of her books has won the coveted IPPY Award for Best Sexuality. And her upscale line of personally formulated sex lubricants, *Slippery Kitty,* is winning nightly accolades from couples around the world.

You can see and hear her on TV and radio, including *Tyra, E!,* Discovery Health, Dr. Drew's *Loveline* and *The Bob & Tom Show.* She's a sought-after speaker and is regularly quoted in national magazines such as *Cosmopolitan, Redbook* and *Men's Health.*

Dr. Sadie is a doctor of human sexuality, having earned a degree from the Institute for Advanced Study of Human Sexuality. She's also a member of the American Association of Sex Educators, Counselors & Therapists (AASECT). ❤

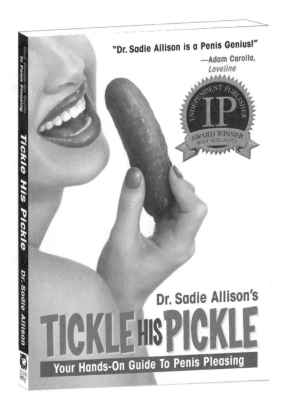

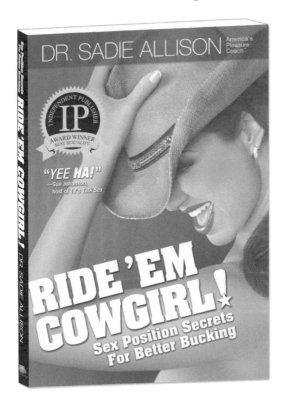

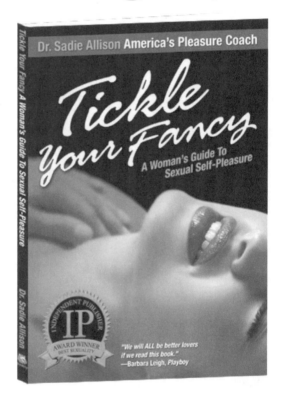

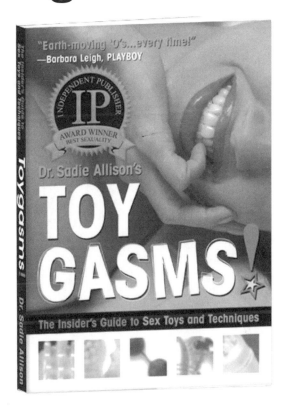

The lube that launches more *omg!* orgasms.

Water-based. Condom-safe.
Stain-free. FDA-Approved.
6 ounce & 2 ounce • *Au Natural* & *Strawberry*
Available at fine sextoy & lingerie boutiques and online.